Nature's Changes

PLANTS
in Different Habitats

Bobbie Kalman & Rebecca Sjonger

Crabtree Publishing Company

www.crabtreebooks.com

Created by Bobbie Kalman

Dedicated by the Crabtree staff
To Charlie, Rowan, Sydney, Julian, and Sebastian—Crabtree's newest little flowers

Editor-in-Chief
Bobbie Kalman

Writing team
Bobbie Kalman
Rebecca Sjonger

Substantive editor
Kathryn Smithyman

Project editor
Molly Aloian

Editors
Robin Johnson
Kelley MacAulay

Design
Margaret Amy Salter
Katherine Kantor (front cover)
Samantha Crabtree (back cover)

Production coordinator
Heather Fitzpatrick

Photo research
Crystal Foxton

Consultant
Patricia Loesche, Ph.D., Animal Behavior Program,
Department of Psychology, University of Washington

Illustrations
Barbara Bedell: pages 6 (sun), 12, 30, 31
Antoinette "Cookie" Bortolon: page 10
Katherine Kantor: page 6 (close-up of leaves)
Bonna Rouse: pages 4, 5, 6 (flower), 15, 16, 18, 22
Margaret Amy Salter: page 6 (magnifying glass)

Photographs
iStockphoto.com: Loic Bernard: page 31 (top left); Marje Cannon:
    page 31 (middle right); Jonathan Cook: page 24; Scott Garrett:
    page 17 (left); Muriel Lasure: page 17 (right); Brian Morrison:
    page 30 (middle bottom); Walter Oppel: page 30 (right); Paul Senyszyn:
    page 11 (bottom); Todd Smith: page 11 (top); Daniel Tang:
    pages 8 (bottom right), 31 (bottom left); Michael Westhoff: page 18
Photo Researchers, Inc.: Geoffrey Bryant: page 19; Carlyn Iverson: page 15;
    Patrick J. Lynch: page 23
Visuals Unlimited: David Cavagnaro: page 14; John Sohlden: page 22
Other images by Corbis, Corel, Creatas, Digital Stock, Digital Vision,
    Eyewire, Photodisc, and TongRo Image Stock

Crabtree Publishing Company

www.crabtreebooks.com   1-800-387-7650

Copyright © **2006 CRABTREE PUBLISHING COMPANY.**
All rights reserved. No part of this publication may be
reproduced, stored in a retrieval system or be transmitted in
any form or by any means, electronic, mechanical, photocopying,
recording, or otherwise, without the prior written permission
of Crabtree Publishing Company. In Canada: We acknowledge
the financial support of the Government of Canada through the
Book Publishing Industry Development Program (BPIDP) for our
publishing activities.

Cataloging-in-Publication Data
Kalman, Bobbie.
    Plants in different habitats / Bobbie Kalman & Rebecca Sjonger.
        p. cm. -- (Nature's changes)
    Includes index.
    ISBN-13: 978-0-7787-2282-3 (rlb)
    ISBN-10: 0-7787-2282-1 (rlb)
    ISBN-13: 978-0-7787-2316-5 (pbk)
    ISBN-10: 0-7787-2316-X (pbk)
    1. Plant ecophysiology--Juvenile literature. I. Sjonger, Rebecca.
    II. Title. III. Series.
    QK717.K35 2006
    581.7--dc22   2005036717
                                                                          LC

**Published in
the United States**
PMB 16A
350 Fifth Ave.
Suite 3308
New York, NY
10118

**Published
in Canada**
616 Welland Ave.
St. Catharines, Ontario
L2M 5V6

**Published in the
United Kingdom**
White Cross Mills
High Town, Lancaster
LA1 4XS

**Published
in Australia**
386 Mt. Alexander Rd.
Ascot Vale (Melbourne)
VIC 3032

Contents

What are plants?

Plants are living things. They make their own food using air, sunlight, and water. Many plants grow from **seeds**. Most plants are **flowering plants**. Flowering plants grow one or more flowers. Sunflowers, tomato plants, and roses are types of flowering plants. Other plants do not grow flowers. Grasses and **mosses** are some plants that do not grow flowers.

*There are hundreds of thousands of **species**, or types, of plants growing on Earth. These clovers are common flowering plants.*

Plant parts

Plants have different shapes and sizes. They all have the same main parts, however. **Roots**, **stems**, and **leaves** are plant parts that work together to keep plants alive. Roots hold plants firmly in **soil**. They also take in water from soil and store food. Water and food travel through stems to the different parts of plants. Plants make food in their leaves.

*Flowers contain **pollen**. Pollen is a powdery substance that flowers need to make seeds.*

The stem holds a plant upright.

Leaves are usually green.

Most plants have roots that grow under ground.

Photosynthesis

Green plants are the only living things that can make their own food! They make food using sunlight. Using sunlight to make food is called **photosynthesis**. Green plants have a substance in their leaves called **chlorophyll**. Chlorophyll **absorbs**, or takes in, sunlight. It mixes sunlight with water and air. The plant makes food from this mixture.

*Leaves take in **carbon dioxide**. Carbon dioxide is a gas found in air.*

Gases enter and exit plants through tiny holes in the leaves of the plants.

*When plants make food, the leaves let out **oxygen**. Oxygen is a gas in air that people and animals need to breathe.*

Using nutrients

Plants need water and **nutrients** to survive. Nutrients are natural substances that living things need to grow and stay healthy. Some nutrients are in soil. As water moves through soil, nutrients **dissolve** in the water. A plant takes in the water and nutrients through its roots. The plant uses these nutrients during photosynthesis.

The roots of these young plants absorb water and nutrients from the soil.

Plant habitats

Plants are found all over the world. They grow in different **habitats**. A habitat is the natural place where a plant or an animal lives. Different habitats have different temperatures and weather. Some plant habitats are shown on these pages.

Boreal forests are huge forests with many trees. They grow in places that have long, cold winters and short, cool summers.

Broadleaved forests grow in areas that have four seasons. These forests are made up of trees such as maple trees, oak trees, and elm trees.

Tropical rain forests grow in hot areas. They receive a lot of rain.

Grasslands *are flat areas where many types of grasses grow. These habitats receive little rain or snow.*

Deserts *receive less than ten inches (25 cm) of rain or snow in one year. Most deserts are very hot.*

*Most of the plants in the **Polar Regions** grow on the **tundra**. The tundra is a large, flat area of land with almost no trees.*

Mountains *are large peaks on Earth's surface. The weather in mountain habitats is often windy and chilly. Few plants grow on high mountains.*

*Water that sits on land for at least part of the year creates a soggy habitat called a **wetland**.*

*Bodies of water such as lakes, ponds, rivers, and streams are **freshwater** habitats.*

9

Boreal forest plants

Most plants in boreal forests are **coniferous trees** or "conifers." Conifers are suited to their cold habitats. Their seeds grow in **cones**. Cones are hard coverings that protect the seeds from cold weather.

Green year round

Most conifers are **evergreens**. Evergreens are plants that keep their leaves in cold weather. Conifers keep their leaves because growing new ones takes a lot of energy!

Pine trees are often found in boreal forests.

Moss is one of the few small plants that grows in boreal forests.

Waxy leaves

Boreal forests can be very dry. A lot of the water in boreal forests is frozen as snow and ice. Conifers have needle-like leaves, shown right, that are covered in a waxy coating. The coating helps these trees keep in the water they need to survive.

During winter, snow covers boreal forests. Heavy snow can break tree branches. Conifers are narrow at the top and wide at the bottom. Their shape causes heavy snow to slide off the trees.

Broadleaved forest plants

Broadleaved forests are made up mainly of **broadleaved trees**. The leaves of broadleaved trees are flat and wide. In areas where the seasons change, broadleaved trees grow leaves in spring, become taller in summer, lose their leaves in autumn, and are **dormant**, or inactive, during winter.

Winter is coming

In autumn, the days become short and cold. Broadleaved trees shed their leaves to save energy. The large leaves use a lot of energy from the trees. The tiny holes in the leaves let off a lot of water.

Without the leaves, the trees can hold in the nutrients, food, and water they need to stay alive.

Changing in spring

After trees lose their leaves, the dead leaves on the forest floor add nutrients to the soil. These nutrients help many plants grow in broadleaved forests. In spring, the trees begin to grow leaves.

Small plants, such as **shrubs**, **sprout** in spring. They grow leaves and flowers. The plants make as much food as possible before the trees above them fill in with leaves. The leaves block most of the sun's rays from reaching the forest floor.

Small plants that live on the forest floor have flowers only in spring. In summer, they survive in the shade but no longer have flowers.

Tropical rainforest plants

These vines are called lianas. They climb up rainforest trees to reach sunlight.

Many plants grow in warm, wet, tropical rain forests. Vines are common tropical rainforest plants. Like trees, vines grow thick stems. The stems are not strong enough to reach the sunlight on their own, however. The vines grow upward by winding around trees, using them as supports. Over time, the stems of vines grow so long that they reach the treetops and absorb the sunlight they need to survive.

Not many nutrients

To grow, plants need nutrients. The soil in tropical rain forests does not have many of the nutrients plants need. The nutrients are washed away by heavy rain. Only the top layer of soil has nutrients. To absorb these nutrients, many tropical rainforest plants have roots that spread out sideways in the soil instead of growing down deep into the soil.

Air plants

Epiphytes are air plants. Their roots do not grow in soil. Epiphytes grow from seeds, which are scattered by wind. Some seeds land in the cracks and hollows of trees. Epiphytes grow from the seeds that land on the trees. Some of an epiphyte's roots grasp the trees. Other roots grow out into the moist air. The roots take in water and nutrients from the air. The epiphytes shown here are orchids.

Grassland plants

Most grassland plants are types of grasses. Grasses are well suited to the dry conditions in grasslands. Their roots spread out under ground in order to take in the water they need to survive. The roots of grass plants can be much longer than the grass stems growing above the ground.

Goldenrod is a flowering plant that grows in some grasslands.

These red foxes are living in a grassland.

16

Hardy trees

Most trees cannot grow in dry grasslands called **savannas**. A few types of trees are suited to living in dry places, however. Grassland trees often have small, leathery leaves. These kinds of leaves store water, keeping the trees from drying out.

Frequent fires

Very hot, dry conditions can cause fires on grasslands. Flames may burn the top parts of grasses, but the roots are not harmed, so the grasses stay alive. Plants such as some eucalyptuses grow in the ashes left behind by fires.

*Baobabs are another type of tree that grow in some grasslands. They are **fire resistant** trees. They burn much more slowly than other plants do.*

The leaves of acacia trees release very little water.

Desert plants

Many desert plants have shallow roots that grow out to the sides. Shallow roots take in more water. Desert plants often have tough, waxy leaves that hold in water. Tiny hairs cover the surfaces of the leaves to shade and protect them from the hot sun. To save water, desert plants may drop their leaves or allow them to dry out.

Common cacti

Cacti are common plants in North American deserts. These plants have no leaves, so they lose very little water. Cacti store nearly all the water they absorb. Cacti store water in their thick stems.

This large cactus is called a saguaro.

Desert defenses

Some desert animals survive by drinking the water stored in desert plants. They sometimes damage the plants to reach the water. Some desert plants have defenses against thirsty animals, however. Cacti have sharp **spines**, or hard, pointed needles, on their stems. The spines stop animals from biting into the plants. Plants called living stones, shown below, have **camouflage**. Camouflage is colors, textures, or patterns that help plants blend in with their surroundings. Living stones blend in with rocks and pebbles on the ground so animals cannot see them.

Polar plants

No plants can grow at the **North Pole** or the **South Pole**. The ground in these areas is always covered with ice and snow. In summer, a few plants grow at the edges of the snow-covered areas, however.

The tundra

The tundra is land north of the boreal forests. The tundra is frozen in winter, but in summer, the top layer of soil thaws. Below the soil is **permafrost**, or a layer of ground that is frozen year round. Only plants with shallow roots can grow in the soil.

Plants that live in the Polar Regions often grow low to the ground. They may also grow in rounded clumps. The sizes and shapes of polar plants help them avoid being damaged by strong winds.

Tundra plants

Plants such as saxifrage, grasses, and shrubs grow well on the tundra. They are often inactive during the long, cold winters. When the warmer days of summer arrive, the plants grow quickly.

Tundra plants, such as this dwarf willow herb, have very little time to grow each year.

Antarctic plants

The **continent** of Antarctica is surrounded by the Southern Ocean. The chilly ocean waters are warmer than the land! Mosses and a few flowering plants grow on the rocky coastline that is warmed by the ocean. Plants cannot grow on the frozen, icy ground found farther away from the coast.

Mountain plants

In mountain habitats, different plants grow at different spots on the mountains. Mosses grow near the tops of mountains. Farther down the mountains, the weather is warmer and wetter. Grasses and small plants grow there. Near the bottom of mountains, boreal forests grow. Broadleaved forests often grow at the bottom of mountains.

The tree line

Plants do not grow on the tops of the highest mountains. Trees grow up the sides of mountains but only to certain heights. The highest point where trees grow on a mountain is called the **tree line**. Trees growing at the tree line do not make up thick forests. They grow far apart from one another.

The trees in this picture are growing at the tree line. Strong winds on mountains prevent the trees from growing tall and straight.

Protected leaves

Like the leaves of many desert plants, the leaves of mountain plants are often thick and waxy. The mountain cranberries in the picture above have thick, waxy leaves. Some mountain plant leaves are covered with tiny hairs. The hairs help keep the plants from freezing. The leaves of some mountain plants are both waxy and hairy.

Freshwater plants

Some plants are **aquatic**. Aquatic plants live on, in, or near water. These plants often have short roots because there is always water near where they live. Aquatic plants such as cattails and duckweeds grow in freshwater habitats.

Sun seekers

Like other plants, aquatic plants need sunlight to make food. Parts of some aquatic plants grow above the surface of the water so that the sun's rays can shine on them. Other aquatic plants grow beneath the surface of the water. These plants must grow close enough to the water's surface to absorb sunlight, however.

These cattails are growing in a freshwater pond.

Water lilies often grow on the edges of lakes and ponds. A water lily has a long, sturdy stem that reaches from the plant's roots to the surface of the water. The plant's leaves and flowers grow above the water's surface. A water lily's leaves are large. The leaves have waxy coatings that keep them from becoming damaged by water.

Wetland plants

Reeds are types of grasses that grow in water.

Certain plants grow well in wetlands. Reeds and **sedges** are common wetland plants. Many of these plants have some parts that grow under water and other parts that grow above water. The plants have hollow tubes in their stems. The tubes carry air from the parts that are above water to the parts that are below water.

Hungry plants

The soil in some wetlands does not contain nutrients. Some plants in these habitats get the nutrients they need by eating insects! A pitcher plant, shown right, is able to trap insects. It uses special liquids to dissolve its food, which it then absorbs like water.

Salty trees

Mangrove trees grow in swampy wetlands
next to oceans. The water these plants absorb
is **salt water**, or water that contains salt. The
trees cannot use the salt. They release the salt
through their leaves. Mangrove trees have two
sets of roots. Some hold the trees firmly in the
ground, whereas others stick out of the water.
The roots that grow out of the water take in
the air that the plant needs to survive.

Native plants

Certain plants that grow naturally in an area without help from people are called **native plants**. The native plants in an area are well suited to the temperatures, rainfall, and sunshine in their habitats.

Many animals rely on native plants for food and shelter. Indian grass, sunflowers, woodland sedges, and certain species of lilies are just a few plants that are native to different North American habitats.

These sunflowers are native plants in many grassland habitats. Sunflower seeds provide food for birds and other animals. People also use sunflower seeds in many ways.

Newcomers

Introduced plants can sometimes threaten native plant habitats. An introduced plant is a plant that does not normally live in a habitat. These plants have been placed in the habitat by people, by birds dropping seeds, or by the wind.

Taking over

Introduced plants often grow quickly in their new habitats and use up the nutrients, water, and space. The native plants that grow in the same habitats may then not have enough nutrients, water, space, and sunlight to grow properly. The animals that rely on native plants for food and shelter may find themselves without food or places to live.

This purple loosestrife is an introduced plant that grows quickly in wetlands. It crowds out many native wetland plants. As a result, animals such as ducks and geese may be left without enough native plants to eat.

Plant and habitat match-up

The parts of each plant help it take in the water, sunlight, air, and nutrients that the plant needs to grow and be healthy. Based on what you have read about how different plants grow in different habitats, match the plants shown on these pages to the habitats listed on the right.

Habitats:

1. boreal forest
2. desert
3. freshwater
4. grassland
5. mountain
6. broadleaved forest
7. tropical rain forest
8. wetland
9. tundra

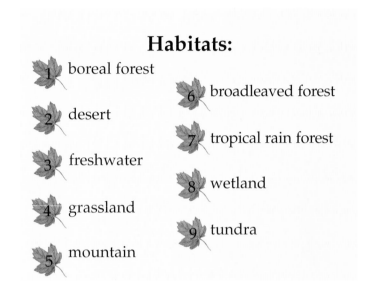

Answers:

1C	5B
2E	4D
3I	9F
6A	8G
7H	

31

Words to know

Note: Boldfaced words that are defined in the text may not appear on this page.

chlorophyll A green substance that is found in the leaves of plants and is used during photosynthesis

continent One of the seven large areas of land on Earth—Africa, Antarctica, Asia, Australia, Europe, North America, and South America

dissolve To cause something to become part of a liquid

moss A small green plant that grows low to the ground and does not grow flowers

North Pole The parts of Earth that are the farthest north

Polar Regions The land and water around the North and South Poles

season Each of the four periods of time during a year—spring, summer, fall, and winter—that have particular temperatures and weather

sedge A grasslike plant that grows in ground that is wet

seed The part of a flowering plant from which a new plant can grow

shrub A plant that is smaller than a tree

soil The top layer of earth where plants grow

South Pole The parts of Earth that are the farthest south

sprout To start to grow

Index

1 2 3 4 5 6 7 8 9 0 Printed in the U.S.A. 5 4 3 2 1 0 9 8 7 6